MARY ELLIOTT NELSON

Mary Elliott Nelson is a Londoner who trained at the New College of Speech and Drama. She has written original scripts and adaptations for companies including Eastern Angles, New Perspectives, Nottingham Playhouse, Oxfordshire Touring Theatre Company, Royal Touring Northampton, Theatre Factory and the Island Players. She wrote and directed *Murder Live!* as part of the Tabs Thriller Season at Theatre Royal Nottingham. Her adaptation of *The Railway Children* was produced at Nottingham Playhouse and London's Peacock Theatre. Other plays include *Don Quixote De La Mancha*, *Hood*, *Arthur the Sword and the Legend* and, for Farnham Maltings, *Miracle on 34th Street*. *It's a Wonderful Life* was premiered by New Perspectives and has been produced by Farnham Maltings, East Riding Theatre and Reading Rep.

Mary Elliott Nelson

IT'S A WONDERFUL LIFE

*Based on the film
directed by Frank Capra*

NICK HERN BOOKS

London

www.nickhernbooks.co.uk

A Nick Hern Book

It's a Wonderful Life first published in Great Britain as a paperback original in 2023 by Nick Hern Books Limited, The Glasshouse, 49a Goldhawk Road, London W12 8QP

It's a Wonderful Life copyright © 2023 Mary Elliott Nelson

Mary Elliott Nelson has asserted her right to be identified as the author of this work

Cover image by Rebecca Pitt

Designed and typeset by Nick Hern Books, London
Printed in Great Britain by Mimeo Ltd, Huntingdon, Cambridgeshire PE29 6XX

A CIP catalogue record for this book is available from the British Library

ISBN 978 1 83904 278 2

www.nickhernbooks.co.uk/environmental-policy

This adaptation of *It's A Wonderful life* was commissioned by New Perspectives Theatre Company and first performed by them at the Old Library, Mansfield, on 6 December 2000. The cast was as follows:

ACTOR 1	Will Gregson
ACTOR 2	Cerianne Roberts
ACTOR 3	David Matthews
ACTOR 4	Michael Strobel
Director	Gavin Stride
Stage Manager	Elb Hall

The play was revived at Reading Rep Theatre on 30 November 2023. The cast was as follows:

GEORGE	Mark Desebrock
ANGEL JOE/SAM/MR GOWER/ POTTER/ED/WELCH/BERT	Eugene Evans
ANGEL CLARISSA/MARY	Orla O'Sullivan
ANGEL GLORIA/VIOLET/ AUNT DILLY/ HARRIET/ MRS DAVIES/MRS MARTINI	Charlotte Warner
Directors	Paul Stacey
	Chris Cuming
Designer	Libby Todd
Sound Designer	Julian Starr
Lighting Designer	Aaron J Dootson
Costume Supervisor	Molly Fraser
Accent Coach	Josh Mathieson
Stage Manager	Eleanor Walton
Assistant Stage Manager	Jamie Kubisch-Wiles
Production Manager	Jordan Harris
Associate Production Manager	Elese Palmer

Author's Note

This adaptation is for four actors, three of whom play multiple characters, as suggested over the page. It is written for three male and one female actor, but can be altered to two of each. Uncle Billy can become Aunt Dilly without any further alteration. Some male characters would then be played by a female actor but played as men. Gloria the angel can be played by a male actor, as can some of the female townspeople in the crowd scenes. The angels become the townspeople to help Clarissa learn George Bailey's story, but the characters they take on are played for real.

The characters can also be divided between more actors in a larger company, and this has been done successfully, especially in the East Riding Theatre production directed by Jake Smith, which also used children to play the young George, Billy, Sam, Violet and Mary in the early scenes.

The stage directions in this script are specific to the production at the Old Library, Mansfield, directed by Gavin Stride, but the play can, of course, be produced in a more conventional configuration, as traverse or fourth-wall theatre.

M.E.N.

Characters

Actor 1
GEORGE BAILEY

Actor 2
CLARISSA, *George's guardian angel*
MARY
VIOLET
and others

Actor 3
ANGEL GLORIA
UNCLE BILLY (*or* AUNT DILLY)
SAM
MR MARTINI
and others

Actor 4
ANGEL JOSEPH
MR POTTER
BERT THE COP
HARRY BAILEY
MR GOWER
and others

ACT ONE

'You are now in Bedford Falls.'

The audience pass this sign as they enter the auditorium.
Bedford Falls is full of the trappings of a small town in America
during the first half of the twentieth century. There are signs
proclaiming: 'Gower's Drugstore', 'John Brown's Hardware...
Boots and Shoes Mended', 'Mancini's', 'Boston Suitcase and
Luggage Co.', 'Bedford Falls Trust Savings Bank' and 'Bailey
Bros. Building and Loan Co.' There are street signs: 'Main
Street', 'Washington Ave.', 'Lincoln Ave.' 'Sycamore Ave.'
Somewhere on or above the set there is a bridge. This should
not impede the main acting area. Interiors needed in Act One
are the drugstore, Building and Loan, and the high school.
Everything else takes place outdoors.

As the house lights go down, the lights of a winter evening
come up. It is snowing and we can hear the wind. The wind
effect starts to sound like the static on an old radio being tuned.
ACTORS 3 *and* 4 *appear perhaps in a separately lit spot. They*
possibly have some listening equipment and/or ledgers... not
too many props though! They are the angels, GLORIA *and*
JOSEPH. *We hear snippets of prayers and carols on the radio*
(e.g. 'Hissing – 'Angel of God, Guardian dear' – hissing –
'George' – hissing 'George Bailey' – hissing):

WOMAN. Dear Lord, just let everyone get on, just for
Christmas...

CHILD. ....Just a little train, please God, and a little bit of
track...

MARY'S VOICE. Help George, please dear God, help my
George...

Cuts into a snippet of 'Ding Dong Merrily on High' (the
'Gloria' part).

JOSEPH. They're playing your song, Gloria.

GLORIA. Same every year, and same joke!

MARTINI'S VOICE. Jesus, Mary and Joseph, help my friend George.

BILLY'S VOICE. We need George. Keep him safe.

JOSEPH. 'George' again? Trouble? Trouble in Bedford Falls. Listen in, everyone.

ACTOR 1 *enters as* GEORGE. *He puts his coat collar up against the wind.* GEORGE *makes his way to the bridge.*

BERT'S VOICE. Never thinks about himself, God. That's why he's in trouble. He needs a guardian angel.

GLORIA. A lot of people are asking for help for a man called George Bailey. We'll have to send someone down.

GEORGE. Water sure looks cold. Wonder how long a man could stay alive in it.

GLORIA. Tonight's his crucial night. We must send someone immediately. Whose turn is it?

JOSEPH. It's been so busy. Christmas Eve is always busy. Most of them are on duty already.

GLORIA. So, who's left?

JOSEPH. Well... the seamstress.

GLORIA. Clarissa? Clarissa Oddbody?

JOSEPH. She hasn't got her wings yet. Maybe I can find someone else.

GLORIA. I know she's a bit scatty, easily distracted...

JOSEPH. Concentration span of a jumping flea...

GLORIA. But she's a simple soul, honest and patient. Might be just what Bedford Falls needs. Anyway, she's available. Clarissa Oddbody!

CLARISSA. You sent for me?

GLORIA. A man on earth needs our help.

CLARISSA. Oh goody! Is he sick?

GLORIA. No, worse, he's discouraged. At exactly ten forty-five tonight, earth time, that man will be thinking seriously of throwing away God's greatest gift.

CLARISSA. His life? Oh my! If I... if I should accomplish this mission... might I win my wings? I've been waiting over two hundred years and people are beginning to talk.

GLORIA. You do a good job with George Bailey, and you'll get your wings.

CLARISSA. Oh, thank you! Oh dear, I've only got an hour to dress. What are they wearing down there now?

JOSEPH. You've only got an hour to save him. If you're going to help this poor man, you need to know something about him.

CLARISSA. Well, yes, I suppose...

SAM'S VOICE. Excuse me...

CLARISSA. Yes... Who...?

SAM'S VOICE. Excuse me, God.

CLARISSA. Oh, it's not for me...

During the following speech the two ANGELS *get ready to become other characters.*

SAM'S VOICE. It's Sam, God... Sam Wainwright? I know you don't hear from me too much but, well, my old friend George Bailey... I think he needs a break...

JOSEPH. You've got one hour.

CLARISSA. So little time to find out about him. If I concentrate... oh dear, concentrate... I should be able to see his whole life... with some help from his friends.

GLORIA. You'll get help.

CLARISSA *is now in the town.*

CLARISSA. This George Bailey is certainly in lots of folks' thoughts.

As SAM*'s voice is heard,* GLORIA *joins in and goes into the town to become* SAM.

SAM/GLORIA. He's a good guy. Could you give him a break, God?

SAM (*now played live by* GLORIA). Hey, I remember when he saved his kid brother.

CLARISSA. Really! This could be useful... go on... oh I hope he goes on... I do think wings would suit me...

HARRY, *played by* JOSEPH, *as a kid jumps up and down and calls out and* GEORGE, *now twelve years old, calls from the bridge.*

HARRY. Look at me, Georgie! Look at me, Sam!

GEORGE. Not on the ice, Harry, it's too thin!

SAM. 1918... no, no 1919. Cold winter, 1919. Me and George, we were twelve. But Harry was just a little sprout, just eight.

HARRY. World Champion Slider! Aaaagh!

SAM. George just jumped right in that icy river. But I guess it's only us who ever knew... (*To God.*) us and you.

GEORGE *runs from the bridge to* SAM *and* HARRY. *He rescues* HARRY. *He is shivering with cold but still in charge.*

GEORGE. You gotta swear...

CLARISSA. Oh dear!

GEORGE. Swear not to tell.

HARRY. I'm cold...

GEORGE. Do you want a larruping?

HARRY. No... but I'm cold and wet and...

GEORGE. We gotta get our story straight... Sam?

SAM. We saw Old Ma Holloway's cat on the ice, and we tried to save her but she fell in and you guys fell in trying to rescue it...

GEORGE. What didn't happen...?

HARRY. George...

GEORGE. Come on, Harry... what didn't you do?

HARRY. I didn't try to be World Champion Slider, I didn't go on the ice, I didn't get saved... but I did get real cold.

GEORGE. Me too. (*Fading fast.*) Now swear... Come on... spit 'n' swear.

They spit on their hands and then slap each other palms.

Spit 'n' swear 'n' hope to die...

SAM. Spit 'n' swear 'n' hope to die...

HARRY. Spit 'n' swear 'n' hope to die...

ALL. Hot dog!

GEORGE (*with his last gasp*). Sam... what are you gonna do?

SAM. On the way home I'm gonna dunk Ma Holloway's cat in the water butt.

GEORGE. Thanks, Sam.

GEORGE *passes out.*

SAM/GLORIA. George saved his kid brother's life that day. But he caught a bad cold... infected his left ear. Cost him his hearing in that ear. It was weeks before he could return to his after-school job.

The BOYS are now recovered, have linked arms and are coming back from school. They stop and stare out at the audience as if watching a carriage go by. Sound effect: horses' hooves.

GEORGE. Mr Potter!

HARRY. Like a king in his kingly king's carriage!

GEORGE. Looks like he's going to see my dad at the Building and Loan.

SAM. He ain't opening an account. He's the richest man in town.

GEORGE. He's the meanest man in town!

HARRY. He better not be mean to my dad!

GEORGE. Don't you worry about Dad. He's bigger'n Potter any old day.

HARRY. Yeah, my dad's the biggest man in town!

SAM. But Old Potter's the richest!

GEORGE. Sure thing… Old Potter's the richest.

SAM. Go to work, slave. Hee-haw, hee-haw!

GEORGE. So long.

   SAM *and* HARRY *run off, perhaps playing at riding in a posh carriage.* GEORGE *goes into the drugstore. This is indicated by shop bell ringing.*

VIOLET'S VOICE/CLARISSA. George was always there for me, God. Now he needs help.

   CLARISSA *can now play* VIOLET.

GOWER'S VOICE/JOSEPH. Help George Bailey, Lord. I owe everything to George.

   GOWER *heads to the back room.*

GEORGE. It's me, Mr Gower. George Bailey.

GOWER (*from off*). You're late.

GEORGE (*putting on apron*). Yes, sir.

   A little girl, VIOLET, *enters. Her main objective is* GEORGE.

VIOLET. Hello, George.

GEORGE (*sullenly*). Violet. Two cents worth of shoelaces?

VIOLET. Please, Georgie. You're nice.

GEORGE. Aww, Violet Bick, you like every boy.

VIOLET. What's wrong with that?

GEORGE (*at arm's length*). Here you are.

VIOLET. Bye, bye, Georgie.

She exits. GEORGE goes to the cash till whistling. GOWER staggers forward. He chews an unlit cigar. His manner is gruff and mean. It is evident he has been drinking.

GOWER. George! George!

GEORGE. Yes, sir.

GOWER. You're not paid to be a canary.

GEORGE. No, sir.

Another little girl, MARY HATCH, enters. She makes the shop-door bell ring twice.

I see you, Mary Hatch. Quit ringing the bell!

MARY. Hello George. My mom says that every time a bell rings, an angel gets his wings.

GEORGE. So, you thought you'd hand out an extra pair, huh?

MARY. It's a nice idea.

GEORGE. What'll you have?

MARY. Pear drops as usual, I guess.

GEORGE. Pear drops! Why don't you try coconuts?

MARY. I don't like coconuts.

GEORGE. You don't like coconuts! Say, brainless, don't you know where coconuts come from? Lookit here... from Tahiti... Fiji Islands, the Coral Sea.

Shows MARY a National Geographic *magazine.*

MARY. I never saw this magazine before.

GEORGE. Of course you never. Only us explorers can get it. When I go out exploring, you watch…I'm going to have a couple of harems and maybe three or four wives. Wait and see.

GOWER. Chattering like an ape, boy. Clean up!

GEORGE. Gee, he's mean today.

MARY. He's not mean. I guess he's just sad.

GEORGE. Sad?

MARY. My mother said his son, his son at college, got sick and died of the flu. I didn't know you could die of the flu. Poor Mr Gower. He only had the one, Mother says.

GEORGE. Yeah. Thanks, Mary.

GEORGE *is stunned by this news. He goes to* GOWER. MARY *exits.*

Mr Gower, do you want something… Anything?

GOWER. No.

GEORGE. Anything I can do?

GOWER. No.

GOWER *is trying to put capsules into a box. He fumbles and drops some on the floor.*

GEORGE. I'll get them, sir. (*He picks them up and offers them to* GOWER.) Here you are, sir.

GOWER. Got enough here. Empty them back into the bottle. Got enough, see.

GEORGE *goes to the big bottle and sees its POISON label.*

GEORGE. Which bottle, Mr Gower?

GOWER. That big one, boy. Are you stupid?

GEORGE. No, sir, but…

GOWER. Take these. (*Thrusting the box at* GEORGE.) Take them to Mrs Blaine's. She's waiting for them.

GEORGE. They have diphtheria there, haven't they, sir?

GOWER. Umm.

GEORGE. Is it a charge, sir?

GOWER. Yes, charge.

GEORGE. Mr Gower, I think…

GOWER. Get going!

GEORGE. No, sir.

GOWER *grabs* GEORGE *roughly by the shirt.*

GOWER. Did you hear what I said?

GEORGE. Yes, sir, I… I can't deliver them. You…

GOWER *starts hitting* GEORGE *with the flat of his hand.* GEORGE *tries to protect himself.*

GOWER. Can't? You'll do what you're told! What kind of tricks are you playing anyway? You deliver them right away! Don't you know that boy's very sick?

GEORGE. My ear… You're hurting my sore ear!

GOWER. He's a good boy but he's sick… but you… you lazy loafer! (*Hits him hard.*) You expect me to go… run errands… What do I pay you for? Look at me, boy. You're a lazy, stupid, disobedient…

GEORGE. Mr Gower, you don't know what you're doing. You put something wrong in those capsules. I know you're unhappy, you're upset. You put something bad in those capsules. It's not your fault, Mr Gower…

GOWER *rips the box from* GEORGE*'s hand.*

GOWER. Why, give me those you cheeky little…

GEORGE. Just look and see what you did. Look at the bottle you took them from. It's poison, Mr Gower. I know you feel bad and…

During this speech GOWER *has broken open a capsule and tasted the contents. He throws the box to the floor and moves towards* GEORGE.

GEORGE. Don't hurt my sore ear again.

GOWER. No... no... What did I do? I could have killed that boy.

With profound weariness he falls upon GEORGE, *hugging him.*

Oh George... George... Did I hurt you? I could have killed him!

He lets GEORGE *go and stands shaking his head in confusion and relief.*

GEORGE. Mr Gower, I won't ever tell anyone. I know what you're feeling. I won't ever tell a soul. Hope to die, I won't.

GOWER. And he never did, he never told a soul. Help him tonight, Lord.

Quietly GOWER *exits.* GEORGE *removes his apron. During the following speech* GEORGE *has changed his school cap for a trilby and put on a sports jacket. He has picked up a large, new-looking suitcase.*

CLARISSA. You know, I like George Bailey. Oh, but there's so much to find out. Did he ever go exploring? Did he marry that girl? Oh my, I hope he didn't marry the wrong one! Maybe that's why... oh dear, I hope that's not it... I really couldn't sort out that kind of thing...

GEORGE (*calling towards the drug store*). Hey, Mr Gower, thanks for the bag! It's exactly what I wanted!

CLARISSA. Well, well... they grow up fast in Bedford Falls! Now, where's he going?

SAM. Hee-haw! That your overnight bag, George?

GEORGE. Sam! Isn't it great! Old Man Gower went right over to Joe's and picked it out himself.

SAM. What, for you?

GEORGE. Got my name right here on it! This isn't just for one night. It's for a thousand and one nights, with plenty of room for labels from Italy and Baghdad, Samarkand…

SAM. A regular flying carpet.

GEORGE. Gee whiz, I can use it as a raft in case the boat sinks.

BERT (*as recalling a happy memory*). Yeah, that day he was set to go to college. All dressed up and his face shining like someone had polished it, like it used to when he was a kid… only bigger now…

GEORGE. Hey, Bert!

BERT. What boat you sailing on?

GEORGE. I'm working across on a cattle boat.

BERT. A cattle boat?

GEORGE. I like cows.

SAM. You're finally off to seek your fortune!

GEORGE. Fortune, fame, high-life, low-life – I'm seeking it all, Sam.

SAM. Well, freshman, looks like you're going to make it after all.

BERT. You deserve it. You earned your college money and your travelling money…

GEORGE. I sure did. Hoarding pennies like a miser in that crummy old Building and Loan office, while old college men like Mr Wainwright here have been living it up.

SAM. Slaving over my studies.

GEORGE. Slavering over all those cute little college girls, more like.

SAM. Aw, there were no girls cuter than we've got in Bedford Falls.

GEORGE. Are you nuts?

SAM. I ain't nuts! You forget, I'm an educated man while you, George Bailey, you are...

He is stopped in mid-sentence by something that he and the other two have seen heading towards them. We cannot yet see it.

GEORGE. I take it all back, Sam. You're not as dumb as you look.

The three men watch in awe as VIOLET *appears. She isn't a little girl any more.*

VIOLET. Good afternoon, Mr Bailey.

GEORGE. Hello Violet. Hey, you look good. That's some dress you got on there.

VIOLET. Oh, this old thing! Why, I only wear it when I don't care how I look.

VIOLET *swings down the sidewalk.*

SAM. How do you like...

GEORGE. Yes.

BERT. Think I'll go home and see what the wife's doing.

Still in a Violet-coma, BERT *leaves.*

GEORGE. Family man.

SAM. Going to Harry's prom tonight?

GEORGE. I don't know. I'll feel kind of funny with all those kids. You're not going, are you?

SAM. Sure am.

GEORGE. Now why would such an educated man go to a silly little high-school prom?

SAM. Mary Hatch is graduating.

GEORGE. Who?

SAM. Mary... Marty's kid sister.

GEORGE. Oh, Mary Hatch… yeah… (*Mimicking her as a child.*) Momma wants you, Marty, Momma wants you, Marty… remember?

During this impersonation MARY *has entered, waved to* SAM, *and walked up to them. She is no longer an annoying little girl.*

MARY. Hello Sam.

SAM. You remember George? This is Mary.

GEORGE. Well… well… well…

MARY. Hello. You look at me as if you didn't know me.

GEORGE. Well, I don't.

MARY. You've passed me on the street almost every day.

GEORGE. Uh-uh. That was a little girl named Mary Hatch. That wasn't you.

SAM (*whisking* MARY *away*). See you at the prom, George!

GEORGE. You bet.

BERT (*narration over action*). So he said his goodbyes to Bedford Falls.

GEORGE (*going to each location in the street*). Bye, Joe…so long, Mr Gower, and thanks again! (*Indicating bag.*)

BERT. Folk didn't want him to go but then they did too because it's what he'd always dreamed of.

GEORGE. Send you a picture postcard, Ernie!

BERT. Don't take any plugged nickels, George!

GEORGE *goes to the Building and Loan as* UNCLE BILLY *emerges.*

GEORGE. Hi, Uncle Billy!

BILLY. Avast there, Captain Cook. You got your sea legs yet?

GEORGE. Aw, Uncle Billy. I'd like to say how much I'll miss working in the office with you…

BILLY. NOT AT ALL! (*Unison with* GEORGE.)

GEORGE. NOT AT ALL!

BILLY. My big brother's gonna miss you though, Cap'n. Heck, I'm gonna miss you. Who's gonna check my ledgers? Specially when Old Man Potter comes calling.

GEORGE. You'll get on just fine with Harry in my chair.

BILLY. He's pretty young for that job, though.

GEORGE. No younger than I was.

BILLY. Maybe you were born older, George.

GEORGE. How's that?

BILLY. Gosh, I wish you weren't going, but I wish young Harry could go to college with you.

GEORGE. Now we have that all figured out. Harry'll take my job at the Building and Loan, work there four years, just like I have, and then he'll go.

BILLY. And then you'll be out of college and back here.

GEORGE. Oh no, not me. Why, I couldn't face being cooped up for the rest of my life in a shabby little office.

BILLY. Oh.

GEORGE. Gee, I'm sorry… I didn't mean that remark, but this business of nickels and dimes, why I'd go crazy… I want to do something big, something important.

BILLY. In our small way we are doing something important. A man wants his own roof and walls and fireplace and we're helping him get those things in our shabby little office.

GEORGE. I know, I know. Gee, Dad's a great guy, and so are you but if I don't get away, I'll bust.

BILLY (*visibly upset*). Yes, yes, you're right. You've got talent, George. You get your education. Why, this town is no place for any man unless he's willing to crawl to Potter.

GEORGE. I better go get ready for Harry's prom. Goodbye, Uncle Billy.

CLARISSA *returns.*

CLARISSA. Oh now, if he's going travelling, I might need some more clothes myself, I...

Dance music.

Oh, oh, that's catchy. So, George is going to spend his last night in Bedford Falls at his brother's high school prom.

SAM. You made it, George. Hee-haw! Eyes peeled for Violet Bick...

GEORGE. Violet... oh well... I don't know, Sam...

SAM. Harry's the guy I want to see.

GEORGE. I thought it was Mary Hatch you were here to see.

SAM. Mary... yeah... Mary's a swell girl. Hey... Mary... Hee-haw!

MARY *makes her way towards them quite slowly, as if through a crowd while* SAM *talks and* GEORGE *watches her.*

Coach has heard all about Harry. He's followed every high-school game and his mouth's watering. He wants me to find out if he's going to come along to college with you.

GEORGE. He's got to make some dough first.

SAM. He'd better make it fast. We need great quarterbacks like Harry, not broken-down old guys like you.

GEORGE (*to* MARY). You... you look wonderful. I'd ask you to dance but I've got two left feet.

MARY. Strange. I've got two right ones. Shall we?

GEORGE. Let's.

They dance.

SAM. Hey, careful with that girl of mine, Bailey.

GEORGE. And I told Harry I thought I'd be bored to death. You know if it wasn't me talking, I'd say you were the prettiest girl in town.

MARY. Well, why don't you say it?

GEORGE. I don't know. Maybe I will say it. How old are you anyway?

MARY. Eighteen.

GEORGE. Eighteen! Why it was only last year you were seventeen.

He treads on her feet.

MARY. Ow!

GEORGE. There now… I told you!

MARY. Two left feet. If you point them at the door, will they take you outside?

GEORGE. We could try it.

They make their way through the crowd, acknowledging unseen revellers as they go.

Thanks for the loan of your sister, Marty… no, no, she'll be fine with me.

MARY. Go away, Marty… I'm getting a breath of fresh air…

They are outside.

GEORGE. Breath of fresh air.

They stand looking at each other.

MARY. What shall we do?

GEORGE. Cross-country run?

They walk.

MARY. Hunt the slipper?

GEORGE. Look! The old Granville House… I could go throw a rock…

MARY. Oh no, don't. I love that old house.

GEORGE. No. You see you make a wish and then try and break some glass. You have to be a pretty good shot, too. Watch, right on the second floor there.

Throws a rock... no not really... towards the audience. Sound of breaking glass.

MARY. What'd you wish, George?

GEORGE. Not just one wish. A whole hatful, Mary. I know what I'm going to do tomorrow and the next day and the next year and the year after that. I'm shaking the dust of this crummy little town off my feet and I'm going to see the world. Italy, Greece, the Parthenon, the Colosseum. Then I'm coming back here and going to college and see what they know... and then I'm going to build things. I'm gonna build airfields. I'm gonna build skyscrapers a hundred storeys high. Bridges a mile long...

BERT. Cop in a small town, you're the one gets called when there's bad news. It had to be me to tell him. He was having such a good time, too.

GEORGE. Are you gonna throw a rock?

MARY throws a rock. Sound of breaking glass.

That's pretty good! What'd you wish, Mary?

MARY smiles and starts whistling whatever tune it was that was playing when they danced.

Hey, I told you what I wished for... now you...

MARY. If I told you, it might not come true.

GEORGE. What is it you want, Mary? You want the moon? Just say the word and I'll throw a lasso around it and pull it down.

MARY. Well, that's a pretty good idea!

GEORGE. It sure is, Mary, I'll give you the moon...

MARY. I'll take it. And then what?

GEORGE. Well, then you could swallow it and the moonbeams'd shoot out of your fingers and toes and the ends of your hair, and…

BERT. George! George! You gotta get home quick. Your father's had a stroke.

GEORGE. What? Did you get a doctor?

BERT. Campbell's with him now.

GEORGE. Mary, I'm sorry… (*But she has already gone.*)

BERT. George gave up his trip to Europe to straighten out his father's affairs and take his father's place at the Building and Loan. Until the time came for him to go to college.

BERT *exits.* UNCLE BILLY *enters, shakes* GEORGE'*s hand and, if possible, shows him to a seat in the audience or as near as possible.* UNCLE BILLY *addresses the audience as the board of the Building and Loan.*

BILLY. Now then… yes… Good afternoon. Yes… Now… gentlemen of the board of Bailey Brothers Building and Loan. I sure hope this is the last meeting that I'll have to chair. Guess I'm not cut out to be a chairwoman, eh, George?

GEORGE. You're doing just fine, Uncle Billy.

BILLY. Thanks, George. Anyhow our main purpose here today is to appoint a successor to my brother, Peter… to Peter Bailey. But first I guess we should offer our vote of thanks to George. Good luck to you at college, George.

CLARISSA *re-appears.*

CLARISSA. Good luck! He sure deserves it!

POTTER (*emerging from audience*). Mr Chairman, I'd like to get to my real purpose.

BILLY. Mr Potter! Wait just a minute now.

CLARISSA. So, this is Jethro Potter, eh? The richest man in town.

At some point during the following speeches, CLARISSA
gives POTTER *some pretty close scrutiny.*

POTTER. Wait for what? I claim this institution is not necessary
to this town. Therefore, Mr Chairman, I make a motion to
dissolve this institution and turn its assets and liabilities over
to the receiver.

BILLY. George, you hear what that buzzard…

POTTER. To the public Peter Bailey *was* the Building and
Loan.

BILLY. Oh, that's fine, Potter, coming from you, considering
that you probably drove him to his grave.

POTTER. Peter Bailey was not a businessman. That's what
killed him. Oh, he was a man of high ideals, so called, but
ideals without common sense can ruin the town. Now, you
take this loan to Ernie Bishop… You know, that fellow that
sits around all day on his brains in his taxi. You know…
I happen to know the bank turned down this loan, but he
comes here and we're building him a house worth five
thousand dollars. Why?

GEORGE. Well, I handled that, Mr Potter. You have all the
papers there. His salary, insurance. I can personally vouch for
his character.

POTTER. A friend of yours?

GEORGE. Yes, sir.

POTTER. You see, you shoot pool with some employee here,
you can come and borrow money. What does that get us? A
discontented, lazy rabble instead of a thrifty working class.
And all because a few starry-eyed dreamers like Peter Bailey
stir them up and fill their heads with a lot of impossible ideas.
Now I say…

GEORGE *comes to the front of the meeting.*

GEORGE. Now hold on, Mr Potter. You're right when you say
my father was no businessman. I know that. Why he started

this cheap penny-ante Building and Loan, I'll never know. But his whole life was... Why, in the twenty-five years since he started this thing, he never once thought of himself. Isn't that right, Uncle Billy? He didn't save enough to send his boys to college. But he did help a few people to get out of your slums, Mr Potter. And what's wrong with that? You're all businessmen here. Doesn't it make them better citizens? Doesn't it make them better customers? Do you know how long it takes a working man to save five thousand dollars? Until they're so old and broken down that they... Just remember this, Potter, that this rabble you're talking about... they do most of the working and paying and living and dying in this community. Is it too much to have them work and pay and live and die in a couple of decent rooms and a bath? My father didn't think so. People were human beings to him. In my book he died a much richer man than you'll ever be!

POTTER. I'm not talking about your book. I'm talking about the Building and Loan.

GEORGE. I know exactly what you're talking about... something you can't get your fingers on and it's galling you... Well, I've said too much. I... (*To audience.*) You're the board here. You do what you want with this thing. Just one thing more though. This town needs this measly one-horse institution if only to have some place where people can come without crawling to Potter.

POTTER. Sentimental hogwash! I want my motion!

CLARISSA. Oh dear...

They freeze.

I have a bad feeling about this. Something's going to happen. Poor old George... I can't stand the suspense... what happens?

They unfreeze.

BILLY. You did it, George! They voted Potter down.

Freeze.

CLARISSA. Whoopee!

Unfreeze.

BILLY. They've got one condition.

Freeze.

CLARISSA. Oh-oh.

Unfreeze.

BILLY. They've appointed you, George, as executive secretary to take your father's place.

GEORGE. But, Uncle Billy...

BILLY. I hope you'll keep me on.

GEORGE. Now, let's get this straight. I'm leaving. I'm leaving right now. I'm going to college. This is my last chance.

BILLY. But, George, they'll vote with Potter otherwise.

Freeze.

CLARISSA. I know, I know... he doesn't go. Oh dear... oh dear! Where's he going now... Oh my, he's early. He shouldn't be going there...

GEORGE *is heading for the bridge.*

He's fifteen years too early...

GEORGE *nods to* BERT *as he passes.* BERT *nods back.*

BILLY. George took a long walk by himself and then he gave his school money to Harry and sent him to college.

CLARISSA. My, that gave me a turn! Oh, but that's dumb luck for George. I know just how he feels. I've been waiting for my wings and, well, I guess he's waiting for his, too.

CLARISSA *exits.*

BILLY. Young Harry became a football star... Mary Hatch was at college too. Only George was left behind, working away at the Building and Loan, and dreaming of Samarkand.

Music of the early thirties slightly overlaps the previous speech. GEORGE *goes to the Building and Loan and, there we see him working and speaking on the phone.*

GEORGE (*on the phone*). That's just fine, Ernie, next week will be just fine.

BERT. Morning, George.

GEORGE. Bert. How you doing? Another five to deposit?

BERT. It's not much but it all adds up.

GEORGE. Sure does. The house is coming along nicely. Why, you and Annie'll be moving in before Christmas.

BERT. Can't wait. Place of our own… why, Annie'll grow about ten feet tall that day.

GEORGE. Better save some more for new clothes, then, Bert.

BERT. See ya later, George.

UNCLE BILLY *enters.*

BILLY. We need George, dear Lord. Keep him safe.

CLARISSA. Surely, he isn't going to be stuck in this office forever. Why…

GEORGE. It's so gloomy in here.

CLARISSA. You can say that again.

BILLY. Your dad used to say that!

GEORGE. But you …

CLARISSA.…Never brightened it up any. He was right to call it shabby. I thought he was being unkind but… oh my!

GEORGE. The carpet's threadbare. It's practically right through just there. (*Indicates the patch in front of his desk.*)

BILLY. Yep. That's where all the folks stand when they ask for their loans and when they pay in their five dollars worth's…

GEORGE. And their fours, threes and two dollars worth's!

BILLY. It's kind of an important place in this town!

CLARISSA. Kind of an important place…

BILLY. Why just think of all the folk who've got their own homes just by standing there!

GEORGE. It doesn't need new carpet… it needs a plaque… no, no… a monument!

They laugh. Then we see them serving a succession of invisible customers. Music may be used to back this.

BILLY. George complained about the office every day. To hear him talk you'd have thought he hated it. To see him work, you'd have thought he loved it.

GEORGE. Mr Martini, buon giorno! Another three dollars, eh? Grazie, Mr Martini. Yes, you might just see me at the bar tonight.

BILLY. Mrs Thompson… two dollars. Thank you so much. Here… (*From pocket.*) Now take some candy for Little Jimmy…

GEORGE. Mrs Davies… another three dollars. Well done. Regards to Bob.

Phone rings. It's HARRY. We see him as he talks to GEORGE.

HARRY. Hi big brother!

GEORGE. Professor Bailey. How's the world of academe?

HARRY. Academe's great but football's pretty good too. I got picked, George… second team All-American!

GEORGE. Well, whadda-ya-know! You go out and slay 'em, kid!

HARRY. Halfway through now, George. Then it's your turn.

GEORGE. Sure. (*End of call.*)

BILLY. Ed, five dollars! You're moving in next week, aren't you? Great day, Ed, great day!

GEORGE *sneakily takes some travel brochures or perhaps a* National Geographic *from his desk drawer or from his pocket if there's no actual desk.*

BILLY. Course George still dreamed his dreams.

Seeing someone, GEORGE *swiftly conceals his daydream literature.*

GEORGE. So, Violet... you paying in today, Violet, or drawing out?

VIOLET *enters.*

VIOLET. I need ten dollars, George. It's amazing what a girl has to pay for herself.

GEORGE. Ten. (*Hands it to her.*)

VIOLET. You can't work all the time, Mr Building and Loan.

GEORGE. No... no, I don't. I don't work all the time.

VIOLET. What are you doing... say... tonight?

GEORGE. Say... tonight? Well... I'll probably end up down at the library.

VIOLET. Don't you ever get tired of just reading about things?

GEORGE. Yes. What are you doing tonight?

VIOLET (*feigned surprise*). Not a thing.

GEORGE. Are you game, Vi? Let's make a night of it.

VIOLET. Oh, I'd love it, Georgie. What shall we do?

GEORGE. Let's go out in the fields and take off our shoes and walk through the grass.

VIOLET. Huh?

GEORGE. Then we can go up to the falls. It's beautiful up there in the moonlight, and there's a green pool up there, and we can swim in it. Then we can climb Mount Bedford, and smell the pines, and watch the sunrise against the peaks, and... we'll stay up there the whole night, and everybody'll be talking and there'll be a terrific scandal...

VIOLET. George… have you gone crazy? Walk in the grass in my bare feet? Why, it's ten miles up to Mount Bedford.

GEORGE. Oh, but it's so…

VIOLET (*as she exits*). If you want to plan an expedition, take a husky!

GEORGE. Okay, just forget about the whole thing.

UNCLE BILLY *is chuckling to himself but does not comment on* GEORGE*'s embarrassment.*

BILLY. For all his daydreaming, George kept the good old Building and Loan ticking over.

GEORGE (*morosely*). Okay, Mr Randall. There's the statement of your account.

BILLY. Mrs Thompson…regular as clockwork… four dollars, is it? (*Fishes in his pocket for candy. But she says something.*) Now don't tell me Little Jimmy's given up candy! Oh, I see, he's going to college tomorrow. Little Jimmy, huh? Doesn't time fly! Well, well…

GEORGE. There you are, Mrs Davies. And don't you worry, Bob'll find some work. You just hold on. You'll be fine.

Phone rings. It's HARRY *again.*

GEORGE. Mr Harold Bailey! We got your wire. Uncle Billy and I will meet the train, okay?

HARRY. Great, George.

GEORGE. But why did you wire us? Come on, Harry, spill the beans!

HARRY. I wasn't gonna say till I got there but… well… I'm bringing someone home.

GEORGE. You're bringing someone… a girl… you're bringing some smart college dame back to funny old Bedford Falls? Do you think that's a wise move? Don't want to put her off.

HARRY. Too late for that. She's your sister-in-law.

GEORGE. My what?… Now, let me see… no, this is my good ear…

HARRY. Your sister-in-law, George… my wife… Ruth Dakin Bailey. Here… meet the wife.

He puts RUTH *onto the phone.*

RUTH. Hello.

GEORGE (*stunned*). Hello. Ruth Dakin Bailey?

RUTH. That's right.

BILLY. What's going on?

GEORGE. Excuse me. (*Covers mouthpiece.*) I'm speaking to Harry's wife.

BILLY. Harry's…???

GEORGE (*suddenly realising that it's good news*). Harry's wife. Well, hello Harry's wife! Congratulations!

BILLY (*calling*). Congratulations! Is she pretty?

GEORGE. Well now, let me see… how do I know? This is a telephone… Uncle Billy wants to know if you're pretty.

RUTH. You'll have to wait and see.

GEORGE. I bet you are. You sure sound pretty. What's a pretty girl like you doing marrying that two-headed brother of mine?

RUTH. I'll tell you. It's purely mercenary. My father offered him a job.

GEORGE (*suddenly sobered up*). Oh, he gets you and a job. Harry's cup runneth over.

HARRY *takes back the telephone.*

HARRY. About the job. It's not settled. I never said I'd take it.

GEORGE. What kind of job is it?

HARRY. Ruth's father owns a glass factory in Buffalo. It's just a research job.

GEORGE. Research, eh? You always said that was what you wanted. When you were blowing up things in Mom's kitchen...

HARRY. You've been holding the bag there for four years and... well... I won't let you down, George. Maybe some time in the future...

BILLY. Come on, George, don't be greedy. Let me congratulate the newlywed!

GEORGE *hands over the phone to* UNCLE BILLY *reflectively.* BILLY *chats away to* HARRY *as* GEORGE *tries to settle back to work. Perhaps some music underscores this.*

Congratulations! You get her here as fast as you can... I'm the same as ever. Nobody changes much around here. We'll see you... both of you... Oh, I can't wait! Goodbye now... Goodbye, Mr and Mrs Bailey!

HARRY *and* RUTH *disappear as* BILLY *keeps chatting and dancing.*

Just when we were down in the dumps, eh, George! We're gonna give them the biggest party this town's ever seen! Business may not be booming but... oh boy, oh boy... I feel so good I could spit in Potter's eye. In fact, I think I will – (*Swigs from hip flask.*) What do you say, George?

GEORGE (*shaking head to decline drink*). You do that.

BILLY. I'm just going to pop over and tell Cousin Tilly...and Eustace and... oh, hang it... I'm going to tell everyone I meet. Just what Young Harry needs. I bet she'll keep him in line.

He exits.

GEORGE (*to himself*). Keep him out of Bedford Falls anyway.

GEORGE *takes out the travel brochure again, but his heart isn't in it and he puts it away. He picks up his hat and is about to leave when* MARY HATCH *enters.*

MARY. Hello George.

GEORGE. Mary. Did you want to…

MARY. I was just passing.

GEORGE. Oh.

MARY. Were you leaving? I'm just out for a walk.

GEORGE. Leaving? No… I… just… moving my hat. I'm working. I don't have time for walks.

MARY. I see.

GEORGE. When did you get back?

MARY. Tuesday.

GEORGE. I thought you'd go back to New York like Sam and Marty and all the rest of them.

MARY. I worked there a couple of vacations, but I don't know… I guess I was homesick.

GEORGE. Homesick! For Bedford Falls?

MARY. It's nice about your brother. Your uncle just told me.

GEORGE. Yeah, yeah. That's all right. Don't you have a walk to go on?

MARY. Aren't you happy for him?

GEORGE. Sure. She sounds like a swell girl.

MARY. It's just marriage in general you're not enthusiastic about, huh?

GEORGE. No. Marriage is all right for Harry, and Marty, and Sam, and you.

Phone rings.

Oh, that darn thing again. As if I haven't had enough of… Excuse me.

He answers it. It is SAM. *We see* SAM.

Bailey Brothers Building and Loan.

SAM. Is that George Baileyoffski!

GEORGE. Sam?

SAM. Hee-haw! Old moss-back George!

GEORGE. That's right, Sam. Old moss-back, George. What a piece of timing. Your girl is right here in the old Building and Loan.

SAM. My girl?

GEORGE. Mary… Mary Hatch.

SAM. Hey, what's she doing in your dingy old office? Fine pal you are. Trying to steal my girl! (*He is joking.*)

GEORGE. Nobody's trying to steal your girl. Here… here's Mary.

SAM. Wait a minute. I want to talk to both of you. Tell Mary to get on an extension. Even your old office must have an extension.

GEORGE (*to* MARY). Here. You take it. You tell him.

MARY *takes phone but moving close to* GEORGE *so they are sharing the receiver. This has got to become sexy proximity or the scene is nonsense. It can be intense as in the movie or it could be fun as they become less and less interested in* SAM's *conversation.*

MARY. Hello Sam. We can both hear.

SAM. I have a big deal coming up that's going to make us all rich. George, you remember that night in Martini's bar when you told me you read someplace about making plastic out of soybeans?

GEORGE. Yeah. Soybeans. Yeah.

SAM. Dad's snapped up the idea. He's going to build a factory outside of Rochester. How do you like that?

GEORGE. Rochester? Why Rochester?

SAM. Why not?

GEORGE. But why not right here? Remember that old tool and machinery works? You tell your father he can get that for a song. And all the labour he wants too. Half the town was thrown out of work when that closed. Why, just today I had Bob Davies's wife telling me...

SAM. That sounds great! Oh baby, I knew you'd come through. Now here's the point. Mary, Mary, you're in on this too. Listen. Have you got any money?

GEORGE. Well, a little...

SAM. Put every cent you've got into our stock, you hear? And George, I may have a job for you, that is, unless you're still married to that broken-down Building and Loan. This is the biggest thing since radio, and I'm letting you in on the ground floor. Oh Mary... Mary...

GEORGE shies away from the phone fearing something personal.

Would you tell that guy I'm giving him the chance of a lifetime. You hear? The chance of a lifetime! Hee-haw, buddies!

SAM rings off and exits.

MARY. He says it's the chance of a lifetime.

GEORGE grabs MARY by the shoulders.

GEORGE. Listen to me! I don't want any plastics! I don't want any ground floors, and I don't want to get married... ever... to anyone! I want to do what I want to do. Do you understand! Do you?

They kiss. Wedding music. They break from the embrace as if waving to friends at their wedding. Freeze.

BILLY (*distractedly*). Oh yeah it was lovely... but I didn't even make it to George's wedding. It was a difficult day. It was the day there was a run on the bank.

GEORGE (*to* MARY). Let's get out of here, Mrs Bailey and start this great big old honeymoon. Here's the kitty. (*Holds up a wad of banknotes.*) Count it, Mary.

MARY. I feel like a bootlegger's wife.

GEORGE. It was a straight choice... Sam's plastic soybean stock or New York, Bermuda... the highest hotels, the oldest champagne, the richest caviar, the hottest music... and the prettiest wife.

BILLY. I don't know how it started. How do these things ever start?

PASSER-BY (*to* GEORGE *and* MARY). If you got any money in the bank, you better hurry.

GEORGE. The bank... why...?

MARY. George, let's not stop, let's go.

GEORGE. Just a minute, dear.

MARY. Please, George... let's go.

GEORGE. There's a crowd outside the Building and Loan... I'll just be a minute, Mary.

GEORGE *leaves her and travels through the audience to get to the Building and Loan. He addresses the audience.*

Hello everybody. Mrs Thompson, how are you? Ed? What's the matter here? Can't you get in? Now why on earth would the doors be locked at two in the afternoon?

BILLY. Then George let them all in. They came in so silently. All the old familiar faces. (*Looking out to the audience.*) Ed and Tom. Arthur Randall and Jeanie Thompson, little Mrs Davies. And... they just stared at me.

UNCLE BILLY *covers his face with his hands.*

GEORGE. What is this, Uncle Billy, a holiday?

BILLY. George... George, can I see you a minute?

They step aside to speak confidentially.

GEORGE. Why didn't you call me?

BILLY. I just did, but they said you left. This is a pickle, George. All I know is the bank called our loan.

GEORGE. When?

BILLY. About an hour ago. I had to hand over all our cash.

GEORGE. All of it?

BILLY. Every cent of it, and it was still less than we owe.

GEORGE. Holy mackerel!

BILLY. And then I got scared and closed the doors. I... I...

GEORGE. The whole town's gone crazy.

Phone rings. GEORGE *answers it.*

Hello? Mr Potter!

POTTER (*on the phone, but visible as* HARRY *and* SAM *were*). George Bailey, there's a rumour around town that you've closed your doors. Is that true?

GEORGE. Our doors are wide open, Potter.

POTTER. I'm very glad to hear that. Do you need any police?

GEORGE. Police? What for?

POTTER. Mobs get pretty ugly sometimes, you know. I'm going all out to help in this crisis. I've just guaranteed the bank sufficient funds to meet their needs.

GEORGE (*to* UNCLE BILLY). He just took over the bank.

POTTER. I may lose a fortune but I'm willing to guarantee your people too. Just tell them to bring their shares over here and I will pay them fifty cents on the dollar.

GEORGE. Aw, you never miss a trick, do you, Potter? Well, you're going to miss this one.

POTTER. If you close your doors before six p.m. you will never reopen.

GEORGE *hangs up.* POTTER *is furious and clicks angrily at the phone.*

GEORGE. Come on, Uncle Billy, we know these people.

BILLY. Was it a nice wedding? Gosh, I wanted to be there…

GEORGE. Yeah…

He moves forward to talk to the audience. The other three ACTORS *now stand close to the audience or move about within it, but turned, facing upstage towards* GEORGE. *They will speak as the crowd.*

I have some news for you, folks. I've just talked to old man Potter and he's guaranteed cash payments at the bank. The bank's going to reopen next week.

ED. But, George, I got my money here.

CHARLIE. Did he guarantee this place?

GEORGE. No, Charlie, I didn't even ask him. We don't need Potter over here.

CHARLIE. I'll take mine now.

GEORGE. No, but you… you're thinking of this place all wrong. As if I had the money back in a safe. The money's not here. Your money's in Joe's house… right next to yours. And in the Kennedy house, and Mrs Macklin's house, and a hundred others. Now what are you going to do? Foreclose on them?

TOM. I got two hundred and forty-two dollars in here, and two hundred and forty-two dollars ain't gonna break no one.

GEORGE. Okay, Tom. Sign this and you'll get your money in sixty days.

TOM. Sixty days?

GEORGE. That's what you agreed to when you bought your shares.

RANDALL. Hey, old man Potter'll pay fifty cents on the dollar for every share you got.

MRS THOMPSON. Fifty cents on the dollar!

RANDALL. Yes, cash!

MRS THOMPSON. Are you going to Potter's?

TOM. Better to get half than nothing.

GEORGE. Tom! Randall! Now wait... listen to me. I beg of
you not to do this thing. If Potter gets hold of this Building
and Loan there'll never be another decent house built in
this town. He's already got charge of the bank. He's got the
bus line. He's got the department stores. And now he's after
us. Why? Because we're cutting into his business, that's
why. He wants to keep you living in his slums and paying
the kind of rent he decides... Joe, you lived in one of his
houses, didn't you? Have you forgotten what he charged
you for that broken-down shack? Here, Ed... remember last
year when things weren't going so well, and you couldn't
make your payments? You didn't lose your house, did you?
Do you think Potter would have let you keep it? Can't you
understand what's happening here? Potter isn't selling. He's
buying. Why? Because we're panicky and he's not. He's
picking up some bargains. Now we can get through this thing
all right. We've got to stick together, though. We've got to
have faith in each other.

MRS THOMPSON. But my husband hasn't worked in over a
year. How am I going to live until the bank reopens?

RANDALL. I got doctors' bills to pay.

TOM. I need cash.

MARY *steps up to* GEORGE's *side. She brandishes the wad
of honeymoon money.*

MARY. How much do you need?

GEORGE (*smiles at* MARY *and takes the money*). Hey, I got
two thousand dollars! Here it is! This'll tide us over until the
bank reopens... All right, Tom, how much do you need?

MARY *returns to the audience.*

TOM. Two hundred and forty-two dollars.

GEORGE. Aw, Tom, just enough to tide you over.

TOM. I'll take two hundred and forty-two dollars.

GEORGE (*counts it out and hands it to actor*). All right, Tom. But your account's still here. That's a loan… All right, Ed?

ED. I got three hundred dollars here.

GEORGE. Aw now, Ed, what'll it take, till the bank reopens?

ED. Well… I suppose, twenty dollars.

GEORGE. Twenty dollars. Now you're talking. Thanks, Ed. Mrs Thompson, how much do you want?

MRS THOMPSON. But it's your own money, George.

GEORGE. Never mind about that. How much do you want?

MRS.THOMPSON. I can get along with twenty all right.

GEORGE. Twenty dollars. Charlie?

CHARLIE. Twenty's fine, George.

ACTOR *comes up and takes money and exits.*

GEORGE. Mrs Davies?

MRS DAVIES (*looking in her purse, carefully asks*). Could I have seventeen-fifty?

GEORGE. Seventeen… Bless your heart. Of course, you can have it.

ACTOR *takes money and exits.* UNCLE BILLY *walks to the front.*

BILLY. I thought six o'clock would never come. We're down to the last two dollars.

BILLY/GEORGE. Six… five… four… three… two… one… Bingo!

GEORGE. Close the doors, Uncle Billy. We made it! We're still in business and we still got two bucks left.

BILLY. I wish they were rabbits.

GEORGE. Let's put them in the safe and see what happens!

BILLY *goes off gleefully with the notes.* MARY *appears at the door of the Building and Loan.*

MARY. Mr Bailey!

GEORGE. Oh, Mary, we made it... oh... Mrs Bailey! Holy mackerel, I'm married! Poor Mary. Hey, we've got a train to catch!

MARY. I guess the train's gone, George.

GEORGE. Oh, Mary, I'm sorry, I...

MARY. Let's go home.

GEORGE. Home? What home?

MARY *opens an umbrella, holds it over him, leads him around the stage as* BERT *and* ERNIE *put together the shabby posh 'Waldorf'. It is raining.*

MARY. Three-twenty Sycamore.

GEORGE. Three-twenty Sycamore... hold on, that's...

MARY. The old Granville House!

Stage whispers from BERT *and* ERNIE.

ERNIE. It just had to rain, didn't it?

BERT. Hurry up, Ernie, I hear them coming!

ERNIE. Sure hope the paint don't run.

As they arrive BERT *and* ERNIE *are ready like doormen to welcome them. They may have a ridiculous Waldorf Hotel sign, maybe a tatty bit of red carpet, comedy top hats, etc.*

Hiya... I mean, good evening, sir and madam.

BERT. Entray, monsieur, entray.

GEORGE. What the...?

MARY (*as they enter the house*). It's okay, George, you don't have to break any more windows. This is what I wished for.

GEORGE *and* MARY *embrace. In the pouring rain,* ERNIE *and* BERT *sing a harmonised version of 'I Love You Truly'.*

*Over this comes music from mid- to late thirties. ACTORS
2 and 3 erect a 'Bailey Park' sign and bunting. GEORGE
goes to Bailey Park. He talks with the other two. BILLY now
narrates.*

GEORGE. Mr and Mrs Martini, welcome to your new home.

BILLY. We need George, Lord. Keep him safe.

*The MARTINI family appear with a cartload of furniture,
bags, sacks, a goat (?).*

George worked so hard all those years. And the houses in
Bailey Park were built, brick by brick, dollar by dollar.

MARTINI. I own the house. Me. Guiseppe Martini. I own my
own house. No more we live like pigs in Potter's Field. We
are home at last.

GEORGE. Enter the Martini Castle!

*MARTINI crosses himself. Then he kisses GEORGE in the
continental style. POTTER appears.*

Okay… just don't go doing that when I'm in your bar!

The MARTINI entourage disappears.

POTTER. Pretty little scene, Bailey, pretty little house. But you
haven't made a dime out of it. You Baileys are all chumps.
Bailey Park? Hah!

GEORGE. How's Potter's Field, Mr Potter? I hear it's getting
lonely out there. Guess it'll be just a field again soon.

*MARY strolls over to GEORGE and takes his hand as
POTTER leaves.*

POTTER. The Bailey family's been a boil on my neck long
enough!

GEORGE. Mary Hatch, why in the world did you ever marry a
guy like me?

MARY. To keep from being an old maid.

GEORGE. If you'd married Sam Wainwright you'd have gone
to Europe. Heck, you could've married anybody else in town.

MARY. I didn't want to marry anybody else in town. I want my baby to look like you.

GEORGE. You didn't even have a honeymoon. I promised you… Your what?

MARY. My baby. (*She exits laughing.*)

GEORGE. You mean… Is it a boy or a girl?

CLARISSA. Oh, that's good news! Starting a family and…

Quietly we hear 'Over There' by George M. Cohen being sung recorded or live or both. As it gets louder, UNCLE BILLY *comes to* GEORGE *with a newspaper,* MARY *joins them. I suggest that* ACTOR 3 *has started singing,* ACTOR 1 *joins in, then* ACTOR 4.

CLARISSA. Oh dear, the war… I forgot there was a war!

CLARISSA *joins in for final line 'And we won't come back till it's over, over there.'*

Blackout.

Interval.

ACT TWO

*We hear, quietly, some WW2 music – The Andrews Sisters'
'Boogie Woogie Bugle Boy' maybe. The three angels enter.*

GLORIA. War.

CLARISSA. I don't like it.

GLORIA. No, Clarissa, it's an awful sign of failure. Do we
know how Bedford Falls got through it?

JOSEPH. Well now, let me see. Everyone plays their part. Mary
joins the Red Cross, she's got three little ones by then, but
she does her bit. Her brother, Marty, helped capture Remagen
Bridge and Ernie, left his cab and parachuted into France.
Sam Wainwright made a fortune in plastic hoods for planes
and Potter became Head of the Draft Board

CLARISSA. That figures.

JOSEPH. Bert the cop was wounded in North Africa, got
the Silver Star. But Harry, Harry Bailey topped them all.
George's kid brother became a Navy flier. He shot down
fifteen planes, two of them as they were about to crash into a
transport full of soldiers.

GLORIA. But George, where's George?... Ah yes... poor old
George.

GEORGE *walks slowly and thoughtfully back to the bridge.*

GLORIA. On account of his ear, he was refused the draft.
George fought the battle of Bedford Falls... air-raid warden,
paper drives, scrap drives... and like everyone else on VE
Day he wept and prayed... and on VJ Day he wept and
prayed again.

CLARISSA. So here we are... back to today... Christmas Eve,
nineteen hundred and forty-five. Oh my, I still don't know
why he's here and there's so little time left to find out.

GLORIA. Down you go, Clarissa. And don't let him out of your sight.

As they exit, JOSEPH *starts the speech then* GEORGE *takes it up.*

JOSEPH *and* GEORGE. The water sure looks cold. Wonder how long a man could stay alive in it.

CLARISSA (*not standing on the bridge, slightly panicky tone*). I wouldn't do that if I were you.

GEORGE *looks round, puzzled. No one is there.*

I need to go back to the start of the day... the start of the day, George.

GEORGE *starts to move off the bridge, heading back the way he came.*

There must be an easier way than this to earn my wings.

As GEORGE *and* CLARISSA *exit,* ACTORS 3 *and* 4 *sing a carol, a jolly one to contrast with* GEORGE's *mood. I suggest 'Deck the Halls'.* UNCLE BILLY *enters with a newspaper with which he conducts the singing,* MARY *enters carrying Christmas parcels.*

BILLY. They're gonna deck the town with a great big banner, Mary, and it's gonna have Harry Bailey's name on it! Hope they spell the name right!

MARY. See you at the party, Billy.

BERT *enters as* MARY *leaves.*

BILLY. Hi, Bert, look at that!

BILLY *holds up the front page of the Bedford Falls Sentinel with the headline, 'PRESIDENT DECORATES HARRY BAILEY – LOCAL BOY WINS CONGRESSIONAL MEDAL OF HONOR.'*

BERT. Gonna snow again.

BILLY. What do you mean... it's gonna snow again? Look at that – (*He reads.*) 'President decorates Harry Bailey'.

BERT. I know, it's great.

BILLY. Great? Everything's great this morning!

>BERT *exits.* UNCLE BILLY *counts the takings in a tatty envelope as she walks along.*

>(*To people in the audience.*) Merry Christmas, Tom…Seen the papers? Merry Christmas, Mr Gower… you coming to the party? See you later, Charlie. Just got to pay in the takings at the bank.

>POTTER *appears carrying a newspaper and heading for the bank.*

>Why, good morning, Mr Potter. What's the news?

>*Grabs* POTTER'*s paper and flourishes it.*

>Well, well, well, Harry Bailey wins Congressional Medal. That couldn't be one of the Bailey boys? You just can't keep those Baileys down, now can you, Mr Potter?

POTTER. Good day, Mr Bailey. How does slacker George feel about that?

BILLY. Slacker George would have gotten two of those medals if he had gone.

POTTER. But his bad ear came in handy, eh?

>*In a fit of triumphalism* UNCLE BILLY *hands* POTTER *back the wrong newspaper, his own newspaper with the day's takings folded inside it.*

BILLY. We needed heroes here too.

POTTER. Pah!

>*He turns away, feels the lump in the paper and looks as* BILLY *carries on.*

BILLY. Someone had to protect us from the profiteers!

POTTER. Profiteers, eh?

>POTTER *considers the situation. He looks at the money and then at* UNCLE BILLY, *grinning smugly before him.*

BILLY. Oh yes… there's some folk who try to make a profit out of anything. Shocking, isn't it?

POTTER. Mr William Bailey…

BILLY. Yes, Mr Potter?

POTTER. Enjoy your celebrations.

He folds up the newspaper and heads for his office or, anyway, away from UNCLE BILLY.

BILLY. And Merry Christmas to you too!

GEORGE *now enters and goes to the Building and Loan. Perhaps he comes on singing.* VIOLET *enters and stands hesitantly at the door.*

GEORGE. Oh, hello Vi. Have you seen this? (*Shows her the newspaper.*)

VIOLET. I've seen it. You must be proud, George. You got a lot to be proud of.

GEORGE. He's quite a kid, eh?

VIOLET. Can I see you for a second?

We see GEORGE *and* VIOLET *talking but the sound transfers to the bank where* UNCLE BILLY *is frantically searching for the money.* BERT *joins him. The sound will transfer between two scenes throughout this section.*

BILLY. Oh shucks… I know I had it…

BERT. Retrace your steps.

BILLY. And the Bank Examiner's due today. He'll want the accounts payable…

BERT. Now look, did you buy anything?

BILLY. Nothing. Not even a stick of gum.

BERT. We'll go over every step since you left the house.

BILLY. George is gonna be so mad at me…

GEORGE (*signs something and slips it into an envelope*). Here you are.

VIOLET. Character reference? If I had any character, I'd...

GEORGE. It takes a lot of character to leave your hometown and start all over again.

He pulls some money from his pocket and offers it to her.

VIOLET. No, George, don't...

GEORGE. Here, now, you're broke, aren't you?

VIOLET. I know but...

GEORGE. What do you want to do, hock your furs? Want to walk to New York? You know they charge for meals and rent up there just the same as they do in Bedford Falls.

VIOLET (*taking money*). Yeah, sure...

GEORGE. It's a loan. That's my business. Building and Loan. Besides you'll get a job. Good luck to you.

VIOLET. I'm glad I know you, George Bailey.

She kisses him on the cheek.

GEORGE. Say hello to New York for me.

VIOLET. Yeah, yeah... sure I will.

GEORGE. Now be sure and keep in touch, Violet.

VIOLET (*wiping lipstick from GEORGE's cheek*). Merry Christmas, George.

GEORGE (*as she exits*). Merry Christmas, Vi.

UNCLE BILLY *enters greatly flustered. He searches desperately, unsystematically. GEORGE watches in bewilderment.*

GEORGE. Uncle Bill...

BILLY. I should have my head examined...

GEORGE. Little late for that... What's up? What's the matter, Uncle Billy?

BILLY. Eight thousand dollars. It's got to be somewhere.

GEORGE (*horrified*). What?

While we see their frantic search, MARY *appears at the Bailey home. Perhaps she is trimming the Christmas tree. Or perhaps she's cooking. Anyway, she's doing something that suggests Christmas preparations. We can hear a child practicing 'Hark the Herald' on the piano.*

MARY. That's very good, Janie. We want it to be right for the party. If you're not too tired you can stay up till midnight and sing carols when Christmas comes. Daddy should be home soon. He's bringing the Christmas wreath for the window.

GEORGE. And did you put the envelope in your pocket?

BILLY. Yeah… maybe… maybe…

GEORGE (*shouting*). Maybe…maybe! I don't want any maybe. We've got to find that money!

BILLY. I'm no good to you, George. I…

GEORGE. Listen to me! Listen to me! Think!

BILLY. I can't think any more, George. I can't think any more. It hurts.

GEORGE (*taking him by the shoulders*). Where's that money, you silly old fool? Where's the money? Do you realise what this means? It means bankruptcy, and scandal, and prison! That's what it means! One of us is going to jail! Well, it's not going to be me!

UNCLE BILLY pulls away from him. GEORGE snatches up his coat and goes home. MARY is on the telephone.

MARY. Yes, isn't it wonderful. We're all so proud of Harry… Oh yes, that's right. It's just like being famous. I'll bet I've had fifty calls today about the parade… No, no, not at all. I'm enjoying it all… Thank you so much. I'll tell George when he gets in… oh, I think I hear him now… I'll be sure to tell him, Mrs Thompson. Merry Christmas!

Hello darling. Did you bring the wreath?

GEORGE. Wreath, what wreath?

MARY. The Merry Christmas wreath for the window.

GEORGE. No, I left it at the office.

MARY. Is it snowing?

GEORGE. Yeah, just started.

MARY. What's the matter?

GEORGE (*bitterly*). Nothing's the matter. Everything's all right.

The piano practice begins again.

MARY. Have a hectic day?

GEORGE. Oh, yeah, another big red-letter day for the Baileys.

MARY. Better hurry and clean up. The families will be here soon.

GEORGE. Families! I don't want the families over here! Does she have to keep playing that?

MARY. She's practising for the party tonight.

GEORGE. Some party!

MARY. George, what's wrong?

GEORGE. Wrong? Everything's wrong! You call this a happy family? Why did we have to have kids at all? And where's Pete? He's eleven years old, he should be helping. Why isn't he helping you? Why, when I was his age I…

MARY. He's upstairs sitting with Zuzu.

GEORGE. Zuzu! What's the matter with Zuzu?

MARY. Oh, she's got a cold. She's in bed. Caught it coming home from school. They gave her a flower for a prize. She didn't want to crush it so she didn't button up her coat.

GEORGE. What is it, a sore throat or what?

MARY. Just a cold. The doctor says it's nothing serious.

GEORGE. The doctor? Was the doctor here?

MARY. Yes, I called him right away. He says it's nothing to worry about.

GEORGE. Is she running a temperature? What is it?

MARY. Just a teensie one… ninety-nine, six. She'll be all right.

The phone rings. MARY *waits for* GEORGE *to answer it but he doesn't, so she goes. He talks to himself as she answers the call.*

GEORGE. It's this old house. I don't know why we don't all have pneumonia. Why did we have to live here in the first place and stay around this measly, crummy old town?

The above speech and the following one may overlap a little.

MARY. Hello. Yes, this is Mrs. Bailey… Thank you, Mrs. Welch. I'm sure she'll be all right. The doctor says that she ought to be out of bed in time to have her Christmas dinner.

GEORGE. Is that Zuzu's teacher?

MARY. Yes.

GEORGE. Let me speak to her.

He snatches the phone.

Hello, hello! Mrs. Welch? This is George Bailey. I'm Zuzu's father. Say, what kind of a teacher are you anyway? What do you mean sending her home like that, half-naked? Do you realise she'll probably end up with pneumonia on account of you?

MARY. George!

GEORGE. Is this the sort of thing we pay taxes for? To have teachers like you? Silly, stupid, careless people who send our kids home without any clothes on! You know, maybe my kids aren't the best dressed kids, maybe they don't have any decent clothes…

MARY *wrestles the phone from him.*

That stupid…

MARY. Mrs Welch, I want to apologise… hello… hello… Oh, Mr Welch, I…

GEORGE (*grabs phone back*). What do you want, Mr Welch? …No, let me tell *you* what I think about your wife.

MARY. George!

GEORGE. Will you get out and let me handle this? Okay, Mr Welch… that's just fine…any time you think you're man enough… Hello… Oh… (WELCH *has hung up.*)

MARY. George, what have you done?

GEORGE. What have *I* done?

We again hear the piano practice.

(*Shouting to child.*) Janie, haven't you learned that silly tune yet? You've played it over and over… Stop it! Stop it!

There is an ominous silence. GEORGE *holds his head in despair.* MARY *watches, afraid for him. Then he seems to calm down.*

I'm sorry, Mary. Tell Janie I'm sorry. Tell them all.

He exits. He is going to see POTTER. *Over his journey we continue to see and hear* MARY.

MARY. It's all right, Janie. Daddy's upset. You can practise now. (*She goes to the phone.*) Bedford two-four-seven, please. (*Under her breath.*) I love George. Watch over him tonight. Hello, Uncle Billy?

By this time GEORGE *has reached the bank and has begun talking to* POTTER.

GEORGE. I'm in trouble, Mr Potter. I need help. Through some sort of an accident my company's short in their accounts. The bank examiner's up there today. I've got to raise eight thousand dollars immediately.

POTTER. An accident, eh? There's a man over there from the DA's office. He's looking for you.

GEORGE. Please help me, Mr Potter. Can't you see what it means to my family? I'll pay you any sort of bonus on the loan… any interest.

POTTER. George, could it possibly be that there's a discrepancy in the books?

GEORGE. No, sir. There's nothing wrong with the books. I've just misplaced eight thousand dollars. I can't find it anywhere.

POTTER. You misplaced eight thousand dollars?

GEORGE. Yes, sir.

POTTER. Have you notified the police?

GEORGE. No, sir. I didn't want the publicity. I didn't want to spoil Harry's homecoming tomorrow…

POTTER (*snorts*). They're going to believe that one! What've you been doing, George? Playing the market with the company's money?

GEORGE. No, sir. No, sir. I haven't.

POTTER. What is it, a woman then? You know, it's all over town that you've been giving money to Violet Bick.

GEORGE. What?

POTTER. Why come to me?

GEORGE. You're the only one in town that can help me.

POTTER. I see. I've suddenly become quite important. What kind of security would I have? Have you got any stocks?

GEORGE. No, sir.

POTTER. Bonds? Real Estate? Collateral of any kind?

GEORGE (*pulls a folded a paper from his pocket*). I have some life insurance, a fifteen-thousand-dollar policy.

POTTER. Yes… how much is your equity in it?

GEORGE. Five hundred dollars.

POTTER. Look at you. You used to be so cocky! You were going to go out and conquer the world! But what are you now? A miserable little clerk crawling in here on your hands and knees and begging for help. No securities – no stocks – no bonds – nothing but a miserable little five-hundred-dollar equity in a life insurance policy. You're worth more dead than alive. I'll tell you what I'm going to do for you, George. Since the state bank examiner is here, as a stockholder of the Building and Loan, I'm going to swear out a warrant for your arrest. Misappropriation of funds, manipulation, malfeasance…

GEORGE *is no longer listening. He leaves the office.*

Go ahead, George. You can't hide in a town like this.

CLARISSA. I see…I see…money… it's just money. Well, that's a relief. At least it's nothing serious. Oh, but I suppose it is serious for George. Going to prison. Yes, that would be serious. But they wouldn't… a man like George… I mean, just for money. Oh dear, I guess they would. I'd forgotten what it's like down here… The time's getting close.

During this speech GEORGE *has gone to Martini's bar and is now being helped out by* MARTINI.

MARTINI. Why you drink so much, my friend? Please go home, Mr Bailey. This is Christmas Eve.

A man just about to enter the bar hears this.

WELCH. Bailey? Which Bailey?

MARTINI. This is Mr George Bailey, my good friend but he…

WELCH *punches* GEORGE *on the jaw and sends him sprawling.*

WELCH. Next time you talk to my wife like that you'll get worse. She cried for an hour. It isn't enough she slaves away teaching your stupid kids how to read and write you have to bawl her out!

MARTINI. You get out of here, Mr Welch.

WELCH. I want a drink.

MARTINI. Not in my bar! You hit my best friend! Go away!

WELCH *leaves.*

You all right?

GEORGE. Who was that?

MARTINI. Don't worry. His name is Welch. He don't come into my place no more. Teppista!

GEORGE. Welch, huh? Figures. Where's my insurance policy? (*Finds it in his pocket.*) Oh, here…

MARTINI. Don't go now. Come back and sit down a little. You don't feel so good.

GEORGE. I'm all right.

MARTINI. Please don't go… please…

GEORGE *stumbles off. CLARISSA makes for the bridge. We hear again the Christmas carol from the beginning of the play and then GEORGE enters as he did at the beginning and goes onto the bridge. He stares down into the waters below for a while. He repeats exactly what he did in Act One.*

CLARISSA. I wouldn't do that if I were you.

GEORGE (*startled*). What?

CLARISSA. I said I wouldn't do that if I were you.

GEORGE (*angrily*). Wouldn't do what?

CLARISSA. What you were thinking of doing.

GEORGE. How do you know what I was thinking?

CLARISSA. Oh, we make it our business to know a lot of things. Your lip's bleeding, George.

GEORGE. Yeah, I got a bust in the jaw a little bit ago… hey, how do you know my name?

CLARISSA. Oh, I know all about you. I've watched you grow up from a little boy.

GEORGE. What are you, a mind reader or something?

CLARISSA. Oh no.

GEORGE. Well, who are you then?

CLARISSA. Clarissa Odbody, A-S-2.

GEORGE. Odbody… A-S-2. What's that?

CLARISSA. Angel Second Class

GEORGE. Oh brother. What did Martini put in those drinks? Why don't you go back through the Pearly Gates and just leave me in peace?

CLARISSA. Oh no, I can't do that. I'm your guardian angel, George.

GEORGE. I wouldn't be a bit surprised.

CLARISSA. Ridiculous of you to think of killing yourself for money. Eight thousand dollars!

GEORGE (*bewildered*). Now… that's the sort of thing… how do you know that?

CLARISSA. I told you, I'm your guardian angel. I know everything about you.

GEORGE. You look about like the kind of angel I'd get. Sort of a fallen angel, aren't you? What happened to your wings?

CLARISSA. I haven't won my wings yet.

GEORGE. So, go ring a bell.

CLARISSA. What?

GEORGE. It's a stupid kids' thing. Every time a bell rings…

CLARISSA. An angel gets his wings. Quite so. But you can't just go ringing it yourself. Oh, dear me no. You have to earn them and then…

GEORGE. Okay, okay. You're the expert. Gimme a break.

CLARISSA. You'll help me earn them, won't you?

GEORGE (*humouring her*). Sure. How do I do that?

CLARISSA. By letting me help you.

GEORGE. Only one way you can help me. You don't have eight thousand bucks on you?

CLARISSA. Oh no, no, no… We don't use money in heaven.

GEORGE. Silly me. I keep forgetting. Comes in pretty handy down here, lady.

CLARISSA (*tutting*). Oh dear, oh dear.

GEORGE. I found it out a little late. I'm worth more dead than alive.

CLARISSA. You mustn't talk like that. I won't get my wings with that attitude. You just don't know all that you've done. If it hadn't been for you…

GEORGE. Yeah, if it hadn't been for me, everybody'd be a lot better off. My wife, my kids, my friends. Go off and haunt somebody else, will you?

CLARISSA. No, you don't understand. I've got my job…

GEORGE. Shut up, will you?

CLARISSA. Hmm, this isn't going to be so easy. So, you still think that killing yourself would make everyone feel happier, do you?

GEORGE. Oh, I don't know. I guess you're right. I suppose it would have been better if I'd never been born at all.

CLARISSA. What did you say?

GEORGE. I said I wish I'd never been born.

CLARISSA. Well, that's an idea. That's a very good idea! I could do that, couldn't I?

GLORIA (*or voice*). Go ahead, Clarissa, go ahead!

CLARISSA. All right… You've got your wish. You've never been born.

As CLARISSA *says this, anything that can change, should change. There should also be an impressive sound effect, like rushing wind. The previous shop signs should change into: 'Dreamland Dance Club', 'The Midnight Rooms', 'The Blue Moon', 'Fights Every Wednesday Nite', 'Pawnbroker & Loans', 'Ma Bailey's Boarding House'. Martini's bar becomes 'Nick's'.*

CLARISSA *speaks to the heavens.*

You don't have to make all that fuss about it.

GEORGE. What did you say?

CLARISSA. You've never been born. You don't exist. You haven't a care in the world. No worries, no obligations, no eight thousand dollars to find… no Potter looking for you with the sheriff.

GEORGE *looks puzzled and cups his left, his bad, ear.*

GEORGE. Say something else in that ear.

CLARISSA. Sure. You can hear out of it.

GEORGE. Well, that's the doggonedest thing. I haven't heard anything out of that ear since I was a kid.

CLARISSA. Your lip's stopped bleeding too.

GEORGE. What do you know about that! What's happened?

CLARISSA. It's stopped snowing. Shall we stroll back into town?

GEORGE. I'll stroll. You can fly.

They are walking off the bridge.

CLARISSA. I can't fly. I / haven't got my wings. (*In unison with* GEORGE.)

GEORGE. / Haven't got your wings. Yeah, that's right. Well, we'll both have to walk into Bedford Falls.

They walk.

Good ol' Bedford Falls.

CLARISSA. Pottersville.

GEORGE. What?

CLARISSA *indicates the new town sign.*

Who's done that? Aw, that's just nutty. Everything's nutty since you turned up. I'm going back to Martini's bar. He's a good friend of mine.

CLARISSA. Well now, I was just thinking of a flaming hot rum punch...

GEORGE. A what?

CLARISSA. No, it's not cold enough for that... I know... mulled wine! Yes, mulled wine, heavy on the cinnamon, light on the cloves...

GEORGE. What kind of a pixie are you?

As they approach the bar, there is a skirmish taking place. They reach the outside of the bar, now named 'Nick's'.

This is crazy. Now what's going on?

An old bum wino is being thrown out. It is a dishevelled GOWER *and* MARTINI, *bitter and angry, is expelling him.*

MARTINI. Get out, rummy! Mr Nick, he tell you not to come here. Get out!

GEORGE. Why... Mr Gower? What's happened? Mr Gower, it's George Bailey, don't you know me?

CLARISSA. Oh my, the apothecary!

MARTINI. Don't you come panhandling here no more.

GEORGE. Mr Martini, what are doing? This is Mr Gower, the druggist. Why...

MARTINI. Mr Nick not let him in his bar.

GEORGE. Mr Nick? But this is your bar, Martini!

MARTINI. *My* bar. You crazy. I work every hour to pay my rent. I ain't got no money left to own a bar. You maybe had too much to drink already. You get away too!

GEORGE. What's come over you, Martini? It's George…and this is Mr Gower. We're friends!

MARTINI. I never seen you before in my life. And if he's your friend you better take off. That rumhead spent twenty years in jail for poisoning a kid. Hey, you know him, you must be a jailbird yourself. You get out of here before Mr Nick come and call police. Get out!

GEORGE. All right, Mr Gower…

GOWER. Lend me a few bucks, son?

GEORGE. I… (*Fumbles in his pockets for cash.*)

CLARISSA. No money, George. Nothing in your pockets at all.

GOWER. Aw, let me alone.

GOWER *wrests himself from* GEORGE *and exits muttering.*

GEORGE. What's going on here?

CLARISSA. Don't you understand, George? It's because you were not born.

GEORGE. Then if I wasn't born, who am I?

CLARISSA. You're nobody. You have no identity.

GEORGE. What do you mean, no identity? My name's George Bailey.

CLARISSA. There is no George Bailey. You have no papers, no cards, no driver's licence, no insurance policy… You've been given a great gift, George: a chance to see what the world would be like without you.

GEORGE. Now look here… Hey, someone's taken Harry's banner… it's gone it's…

GEORGE *wanders bewildered amongst the new signs of Pottersville.*

But where's the drugstore, and old John Brown's Boot and Shoe? Now he can't be gone, he's got Pete's best boots to mend. Why there's no pawnbroker in Bedford Falls… I must have had more to drink than I… where is this?

CLARISSA. Pottersville.

GEORGE. I want Bedford Falls!

CLARISSA. No such place. No George Bailey, no Bedford Falls.

GEORGE. Wait a minute here. This is some sort of a horrible dream. So long, angel, or whatever you are, I'm going home.

CLARISSA. Home? What home?

GEORGE. Three-twenty Sycamore…

CLARISSA *is shaking her head.*

Cut it out! You're… you're crazy! That's what I think… you're screwy, and you're driving me crazy too! I'm going home and see my wife and family. Do you understand that? And I'm going home alone!

GEORGE *runs away from* CLARISSA *and comes to the front of the Building and Loan. It now bears a shabby sign saying, 'Ma Bailey's Boarding House'.* SAM *appears. He is an official coming to close down the business. He works for Potter.*

GEORGE. Hey… hey. Where did the Building and Loan move to?

SAM. The Building and what?

GEORGE. The Building and Loan. Sam? I thought you were in Europe.

SAM. My name's Sam, yes. Sam Wainwright. Do I know…?

GEORGE. Oh yeah, you don't know me. Where's the Building and Loan?

SAM. They went out of business years ago. And now Ma Bailey's on the ropes too.

GEORGE. Ma Bailey?

SAM. The bank has foreclosed on her. The business is bankrupt.

GEORGE. On Christmas Eve?

SAM. No room for sentiment in business, as Mr Potter always says.

GEORGE. You work for Potter? Oh, but where's Ma Bailey? Is she the mother of Harry and George Bailey?

SAM. She had one son. He died young. Accident on the ice. Who wants to know?

BERT *wanders on listening.*

GEORGE. Me! I'm George! I'm her son! I saved Harry, I…

BERT. Take it easy, fella. You'll end up in the cooler with the rest of the drunks.

SAM. Got a good haul tonight, Bert?

BERT. Always do on Christmas Eve. Just put Violet Bick away and she nearly screamed the place down.

SAM. Gee, she should be used to it by now.

GEORGE. Violet?

SAM. You know Violet?

GEORGE. Sure. Why I loaned her some money this afternoon.

BERT. Right. Lots of guys 'loan' Violet money. Don't take it personal, buddy!

SAM *and* BERT *laugh.* SAM *finishes locking up.*

SAM. That's me finished for Christmas.

GEORGE. Excuse me, do you know where Ma Bailey is?

SAM. No idea. She's not my problem. I just have to secure the premises.

GEORGE. Uncle Billy… Where's Uncle Billy? Billy Bailey?

BERT. Hey, you ain't been around for a long time, mister! Why Billy's been in the insane asylum ever since the business went bust.

GEORGE. Bert… don't you know me? You *must* know me, Bert.

BERT. I don't know how you know my name.

GEORGE. You're Bert Bishop. You live in Bailey Park with your wife and kids.

BERT. You seen my wife?

GEORGE. Seen your wife? I've been to your house a hundred times.

BERT. Look, bud, what's the idea? I live in a shack in Potter's Field and my wife ran away three years ago. I ain't never seen you before in my life. But I'm going to keep my eye on you... you're crazy!

CLARISSA *has caught up by now and has been watching.*

CLARISSA. Strange, isn't it? Each man's life touches so many other lives, and when he isn't around, he leaves an awful hole, doesn't he?

GEORGE. I've heard of things like this. You've got me in some kind of spell, or something. Well, I'm going to get out of it... the last man I talked to before all this stuff was Martini.

CLARISSA. You know where he lives?

GEORGE. Sure I know. He lives in Bailey Park.

CLARISSA. There is no Bailey Park, George.

GEORGE. There is, there is! Stop it!

CLARISSA. There are no houses in Bailey Park. You weren't there to build them.

GEORGE. I'm alive and so is Harry. Harry's a hero. There's a parade tomorrow... But they took down the banner... I don't know why...

CLARISSA. Your brother, Harry Bailey, broke through the ice and was drowned at the age of nine.

GEORGE. That's a lie. Harry Bailey went to war! He got the Congressional Medal of Honor! He saved the lives of every man on that transport.

CLARISSA. Every man on that transport died. Harry wasn't there to save them because you weren't there to save Harry. George, you really had a wonderful life. Don't you see what a mistake it would be to throw it away?

GEORGE. Where's Mary?

CLARISSA. Oh, well I can't...

GEORGE. I don't know how you know these things, but tell me... where is she?

CLARISSA. I really don't...

GEORGE. I want to go home. I want my wife and my children.

CLARISSA. There is no home, George... There is no George... so she's not your wife.

GEORGE. Whose wife is she? Tell me!

He grabs CLARISSA.

CLARISSA. Now, now, George...

BERT *comes over to sort out the fracas.*

BERT. What's going on?

GEORGE. Where's Mary? I want Mary!

CLARISSA. She's not here. She left town.

GEORGE. Why would she leave? She loves Bedford Falls. God knows why, but...

CLARISSA. She loved it because you were in it. Without you it meant nothing. She never married. There are no children. Without you, none of it ever happened.

GEORGE. Give me back my family! Give me back my life!

He is becoming loud and violent, so BERT *intervenes.*

BERT. That's enough. I don't know who you two guys are, but I think you should go back to where you came from. You don't belong in Pottersville.

GEORGE. No, I don't belong in Pottersville! I don't want to! Get off me!

GEORGE struggles with BERT and hits him.

BERT. You need a straightjacket. I arrest you…

GEORGE. You can't! I don't exist!

As GEORGE runs off.

BERT. Stop that man!

As GEORGE runs off, BERT fires a shot after him. GEORGE runs to the bridge.

GEORGE. Guardian angel! Whatever you are! Help me! Get me back. Get me back. I don't care what happens to me. Only get me back to my wife and kids. Help me, please… I want to live again! Please, God, let me live again.

BERT appears making for the bridge. It is snowing.

BERT. Hey, George, George! You all right?

GEORGE backs away and prepares to hit BERT again.

BERT. What's the matter?

GEORGE. Get out of here or I'll hit you again!

BERT. What the Sam Hill are you yelling for, George?

GEORGE. Don't… George? Bert, do you know me?

BERT. Know you? Are you kidding? I've been looking all over town trying to find you. Mary phoned and then Mr Martini… Hey, your mouth's bleeding. Are you sure you're all right?

GEORGE. Bleeding? (*Licks the side of his mouth.*) My mouth's bleeding! (*Puts his hand into his pocket.*) A dollar… my last dollar, Bert! It's yours! (*Euphorically he slaps the dollar into the hand of the bewildered BERT.*) Merry Christmas! Mary! Mary!

GEORGE runs off the bridge and goes to the town sign.

Hello Bedford Falls!

He runs around the town or, indeed, the hall, shouting to anyone and everyone.

Merry Christmas!

He greets each location on the street.

Merry Christmas, Drug Store! Merry Christmas. emporium! (*To the bank.*) Merry Christmas, Mr Potter!

GEORGE *goes to the Building and Loan.*

Merry Christmas, you wonderful old Building and Loan!

GEORGE *rushes home. If this is not possible the final moments could be played in the Building and Loan, but home would be nice.*

Mary! Mary! Hello kids!

UNCLE BILLY *is there looking confused.*

BILLY. George, we didn't know where you were.

GEORGE. I wasn't anywhere. But now I'm here. It's wonderful, isn't it?

BILLY. George, the Sheriff is waiting at the office. He has a warrant.

GEORGE. I know, I know. Have you seen Mary?

MARY *enters from outdoors.*

Hallelujah!

MARY. George! Darling!

They embrace.

GEORGE. Let me touch you! Oh, you're real!

MARY. Where have you been?

GEORGE. You have no idea what happened to me!

MARY. You have no idea what happened… They're on their way! It's a miracle!

BILLY. Mary did it, George! She just told a few people you were in trouble, and they scattered all over town collecting money. They didn't ask any questions… just said, 'If George is in trouble, count on me.' You never saw anything like it!

JOSEPH enters carrying a clothes basket full of money. Now he narrates and the others produce voices and vague impressions of the characters as the action begins to fade back into a story.

JOSEPH. And as George Bailey watched, in they came, one by one, with dollars and dimes, whatever they could spare… perhaps a little more… Bert the cop and his wife, Annie… (*As* BERT.) Here you are, George, Merry Christmas!

GLORIA. Ed and Tom…

JOSEPH. And Arthur Randall..

GLORIA (*as* TOM). What is this George? Another run on the bank?

JOSEPH. Mrs Thompson…

GEORGE. Well, hi Mrs Thompson…

JOSEPH (*as* MRS THOMPSON). I got all my neighbours out of bed and they all gave.

GEORGE. Aw, you shouldn't…

GLORIA (*as* MARTINI). I wouldn't have a roof over my head if it wasn't for you…

GEORGE. Mr Martini! Come in…

MARTINI. I busted the jukebox too!

JOSEPH. It seemed like the whole of Bedford Falls had turned up.

GEORGE. Violet Bick!

VIOLET. I'm not going to go, George. I changed my mind.

GLORIA. And old Mr Gower…

JOSEPH (*as* GOWER). I made the rounds of my charge accounts.

GEORGE. Mrs Davies…

GLORIA (*as* MRS DAVIES). I had a little in the biscuit tin. Merry Christmas, Mr Bailey.

JOSEPH. And amidst the hubbub, a cable arrived.

UNCLE BILLY. Just a minute. Quiet everybody. Quiet. Now this is from London: Mr Gower cables you need cash. Stop. My office instructed to advance you any money you need. Stop. Hee-haw and Merry Christmas. Sam Wainwright.

GEORGE. Good old Sam…

JOSEPH. And in the crowd thronging the doorway, a young man in a uniform appeared… a man who had been away a long time…

MARY. Harry… it's Harry, George… He's here!

JOSEPH (*as* HARRY). I got here as quickly as I could. They didn't want me to fly in the blizzard but I pulled rank.

MARY. What about your banquet?

HARRY. Oh, I left right in the middle of it as soon as I got your telegram.

MARTINI. Some wine!

HARRY. Good idea, Mr Martini! A toast…to my big brother, George. The richest man in town!

The others quietly sing 'Auld Lang Syne' as ACTOR 2 *speaks.*

CLARISSA. So, George Bailey learned that no man is a failure who has friends.

Church bells ring out midnight.

GEORGE. Hey, Mary, every time a bell rings, an angel gets his wings!

CLARISSA. Who knows? Maybe it's true.

They sing a full verse of 'Auld Lang Syne' perhaps with the audience. They end by calling out 'Merry Christmas, everybody'.

The End.

www.nickhernbooks.co.uk

facebook.com/nickhernbooks

twitter.com/nickhernbooks